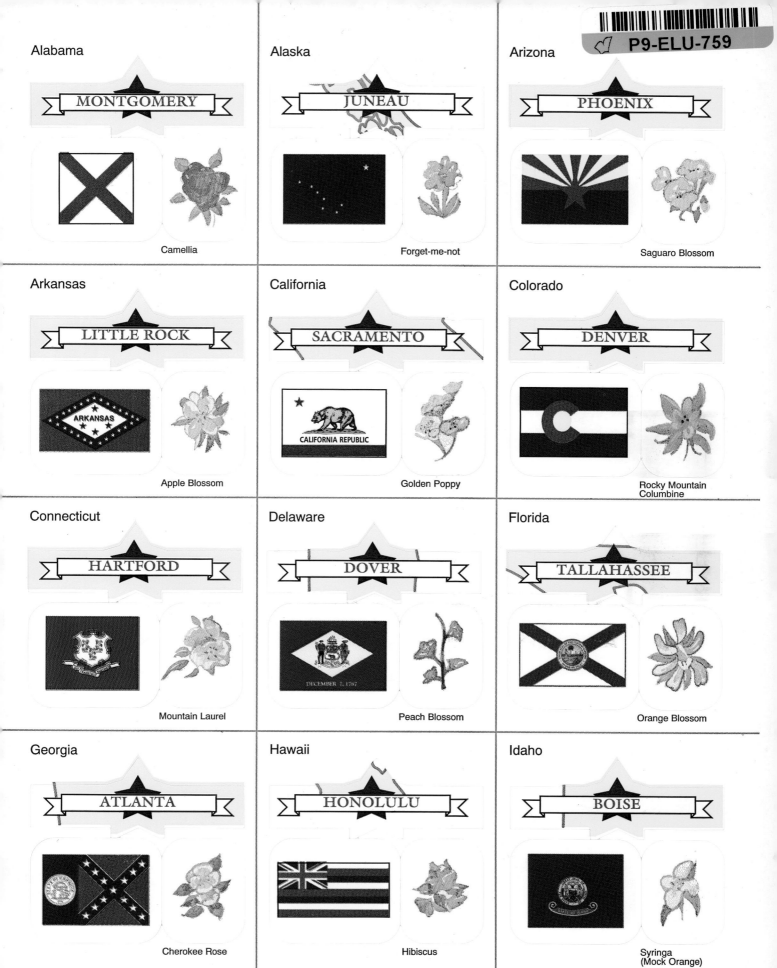

Alabama — MONTGOMERY — Camellia

Alaska — JUNEAU — Forget-me-not

Arizona — PHOENIX — Saguaro Blossom

Arkansas — LITTLE ROCK — Apple Blossom

California — SACRAMENTO — Golden Poppy

Colorado — DENVER — Rocky Mountain Columbine

Connecticut — HARTFORD — Mountain Laurel

Delaware — DOVER — Peach Blossom

Florida — TALLAHASSEE — Orange Blossom

Georgia — ATLANTA — Cherokee Rose

Hawaii — HONOLULU — Hibiscus

Idaho — BOISE — Syringa (Mock Orange)

Illinois	**Indiana**	**Iowa**
SPRINGFIELD	INDIANAPOLIS	DES MOINES
Meadow Violet	Peony	Wild Rose
Kansas	**Kentucky**	**Louisiana**
TOPEKA	FRANKFORT	BATON ROUGE
Sunflower	Goldenrod	Magnolia
Maine	**Maryland**	**Massachusetts**
AUGUSTA	ANNAPOLIS	BOSTON
White Pine Cone and Tassel	Black-eyed Susan	Mayflower
Michigan	**Minnesota**	**Mississippi**
LANSING	ST. PAUL	JACKSON
Apple Blossom	Pink and White Lady's Slipper	Magnolia

Pages 2-3

Missouri

Hawthorn

JEFFERSON CITY

The State Sticker Book

Written by Justine Korman.
Cover illustrated by Jerry Gonzalez and Steve Sullivan.
Spot art by Dick Codor. Icons by Steve Sullivan.
Maps by Jerry Gonzalez. Flower sticker
art by Gwen Connelly.

The United States
of America

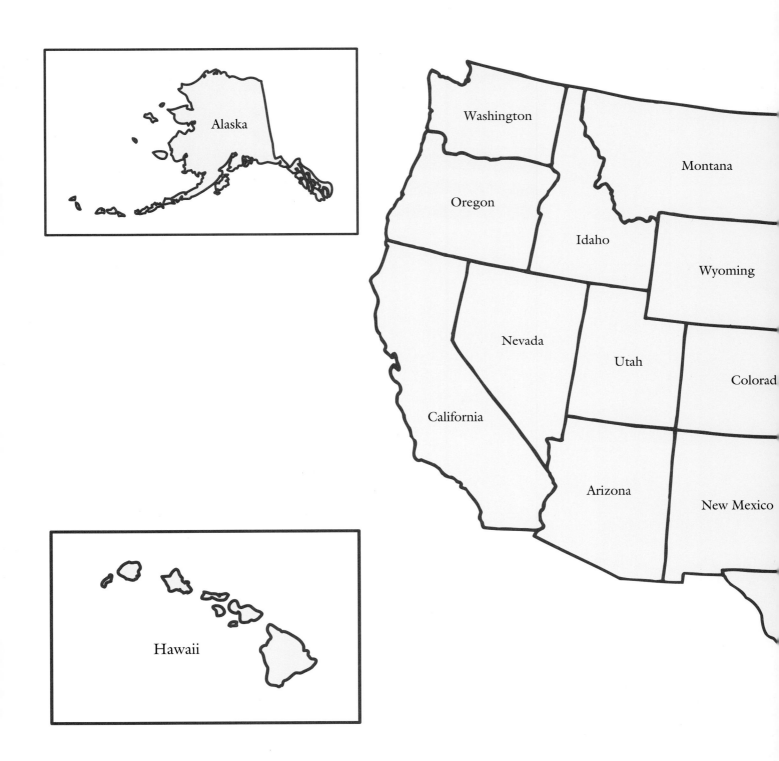

Alaska

Washington

Montana

Oregon

Idaho

Wyoming

Nevada

Utah

Colorad

California

Arizona

New Mexico

Hawaii

2

There are 50 states in the United States of America. Each and every state is different and exciting. And together they make up one great country! Put the red star sticker on your home state. Look for other states you have visited. Put blue stars on them.

Forty-eight of the 50 United States are neighbors—you could walk from one to the other and never even know! Alaska and Hawaii are the only two states not connected by land to any other state. To get to them, you have to take a boat or fly!

Alabama

☆ The Yellowhammer State ☆

NASA's Marshall Space Flight Center is in Huntsville. Because of this busy rocket research center, Alabama is sometimes called The Pioneer Space Capital of the World.

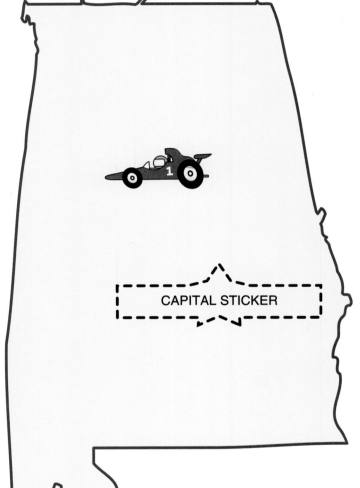

Alabama's Russell Cave National Monument is full of tools, weapons, and bones left by people who lived in its spooky passages about 8,000 years ago.

Camellia

Fun Fact:
Alabama's state horse is a rocking horse!

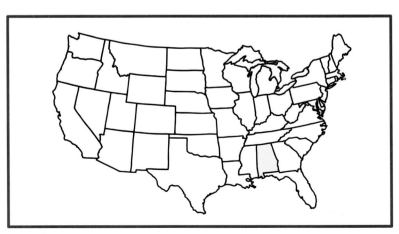

Alasaka

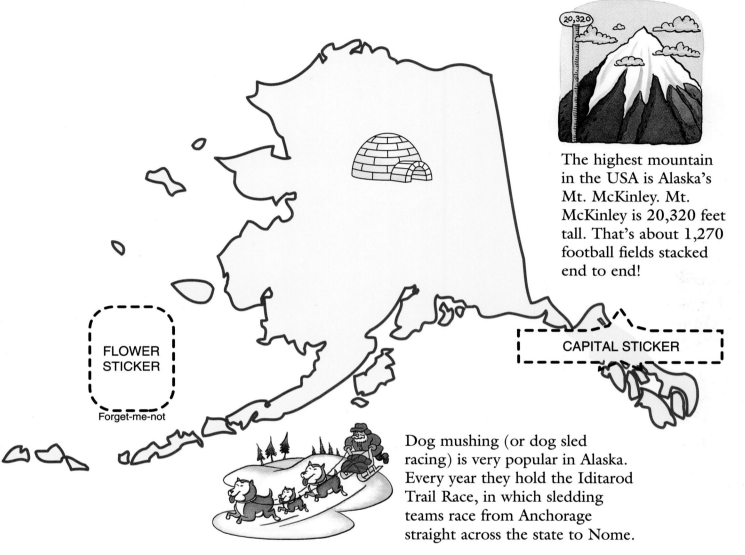

FLAG STICKER

FLOWER STICKER

Forget-me-not

CAPITAL STICKER

The highest mountain in the USA is Alaska's Mt. McKinley. Mt. McKinley is 20,320 feet tall. That's about 1,270 football fields stacked end to end!

Dog mushing (or dog sled racing) is very popular in Alaska. Every year they hold the Iditarod Trail Race, in which sledding teams race from Anchorage straight across the state to Nome.

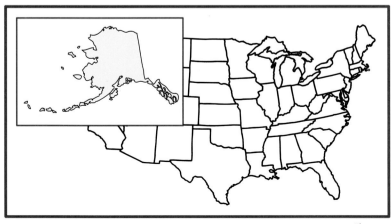

True Trivia:
In Alaska, it can get as hot as 100°F in the summer!

5

Arizona

☆ The Grand Canyon State ☆

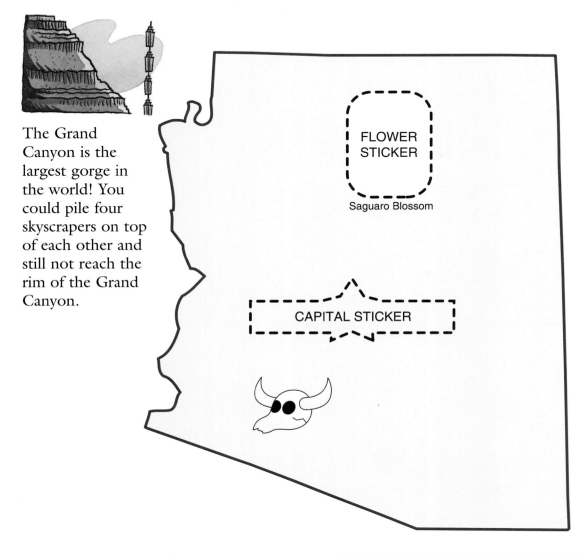

FLOWER STICKER

Saguaro Blossom

CAPITAL STICKER

The Grand Canyon is the largest gorge in the world! You could pile four skyscrapers on top of each other and still not reach the rim of the Grand Canyon.

Arizona is home to the giant Saguaro cactus. These big plants can grow as tall as 5-story buildings and can live up to 200 years! Many don't even grow arms until they are 50 or 60 years old.

Fun Fact:
Roadrunners aren't just in cartoons! In Arizona, you can see them running away from their enemies at 20 mph!

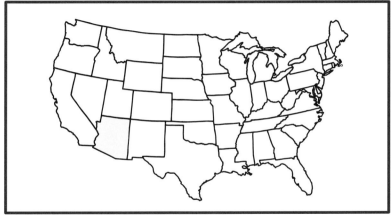

Arkansas

⭐ The Land of Opportunity ⭐

FLAG STICKER

Hot springs are natural sources of hot water. They are found in places where super-hot melted rock called magma is just below the surface of the ground. The magma heats the springwater just like a flame under a tea kettle.

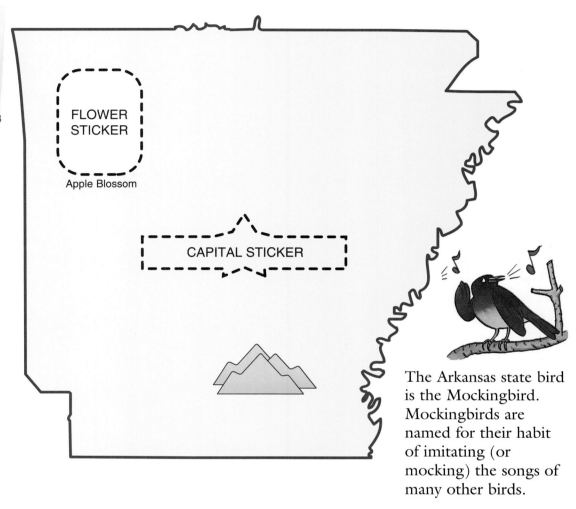

FLOWER STICKER

Apple Blossom

CAPITAL STICKER

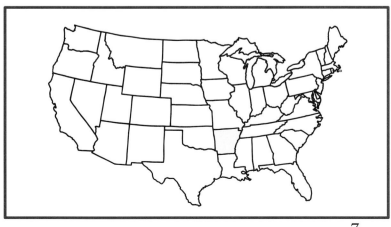

The Arkansas state bird is the Mockingbird. Mockingbirds are named for their habit of imitating (or mocking) the songs of many other birds.

True Trivia:
Arkansas is sometimes called the Hot Water State.

7

California

☆ The Golden State ☆

FLAG STICKER

CAPITAL STICKER

FLOWER STICKER

Golden Poppy

California's Sequoia National Park is home to the biggest living things on Earth. The giant Sequoia trees have changed little since dinosaur days. And some have been growing since the Pharaohs ruled ancient Egypt!

Many movie stars live in California. The most famous stars are asked to leave their mark in the cement in front of Mann's Chinese Theater in Los Angeles.

Fun Fact:
San Francisco's famous Golden Gate Bridge really is painted red!

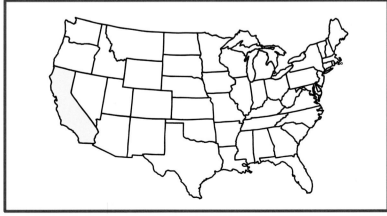

Colorado

☆ The Centennial State ☆

FLAG STICKER

CAPITAL STICKER

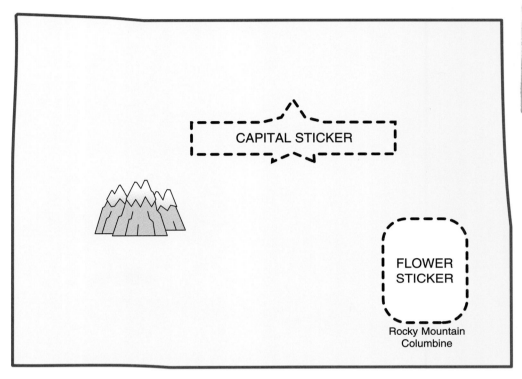

FLOWER STICKER

Rocky Mountain Columbine

Once the Rocky Mountains were full of silver. But people took so much of it, it ran out. Now people come to the Rockies to ski!

William F. Cody was a Pony Express rider, scout, and showman known as Buffalo Bill. At the Buffalo Bill Museum, visitors can trace the exciting history of Cody's life and see photos and exhibits from Buffalo Bill's Wild West show.

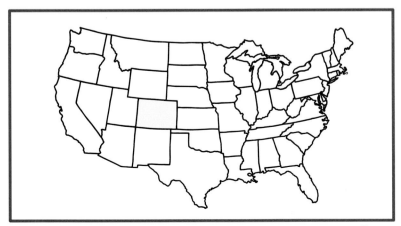

I'M FROM COLORADO

True Trivia:
Did you know that Colorado has an official state dinosaur? The stegosaurus!

Connecticut

☆ The Constitution State ☆

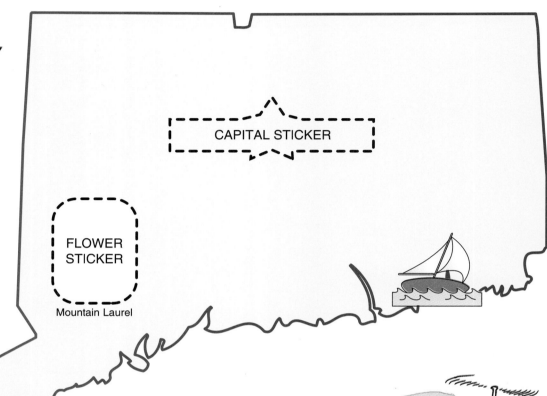

FLAG STICKER

CAPITAL STICKER

FLOWER STICKER

Mountain Laurel

Benedict Arnold, the infamous Revolutionary War traitor, was born in Connecticut. In 1781, Arnold turned his back on the Americans and led British troops in their raid of New London, Connecticut.

Connecticut's state ship is the USS *Nautilus*, which was the first atomic-powered submarine. In Connecticut, people also build helicopters, jet aircraft engines, and regular submarines.

Fun Fact:
Connecticut's state insect is the praying mantis.

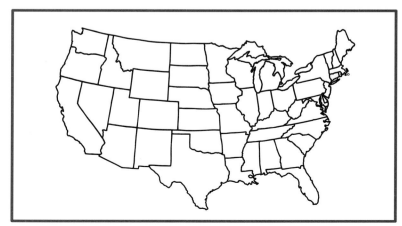

Delaware

☆ The First State ☆

Delaware was named after the Delaware Indians. But it is not an Indian word! The tribe was named for the Delaware River. The river was named after Sir Thomas West, Lord De La Warr. Sir Thomas was governor of the Virginia colony.

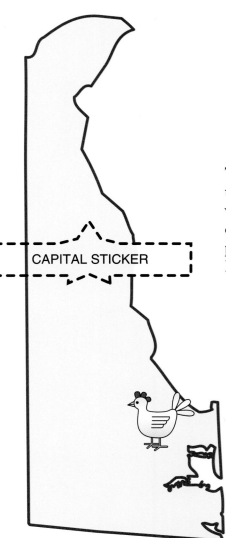

Thomas Jefferson, who wrote the Constitution, said Delaware was like a diamond—small, but of great value. So sometimes people call Delaware the Diamond State.

Peach Blossom

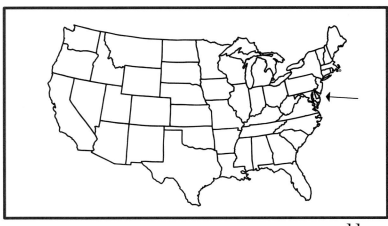

THAT'S ME

True Trivia:
Some states don't have a state bug, but Delaware does—the ladybug!

Florida

☆ The Sunshine State ☆

FLAG STICKER

Everglades National Park is home to over 300 different types of birds. If you go there, you can see pelicans, storks, flamingos, egrets, and herons! But be careful, there are also lots of alligators!

CAPITAL STICKER

On Easter Sunday 1513, the Spanish explorer Juan Ponce de León came to Florida looking for the Fountain of Youth. He didn't find it, but he did give Florida its name. He called it La Florida in honor of Pascua Florida, the Spanish feast of flowers held at Eastertime.

FLOWER STICKER

Orange Blossom

Fun Fact:
Seventy percent of the world's grapefruits and 75% of the oranges in the USA are grown in Florida. That's a lot of fruit!

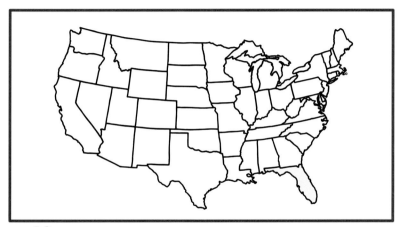

Georgia

☆ The Peach State ☆

FLAG STICKER

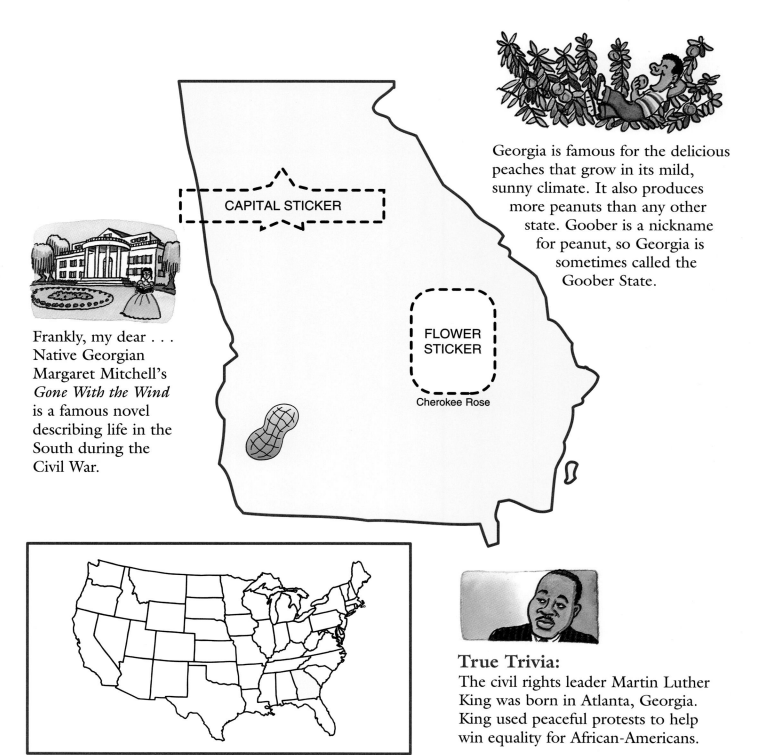

Georgia is famous for the delicious peaches that grow in its mild, sunny climate. It also produces more peanuts than any other state. Goober is a nickname for peanut, so Georgia is sometimes called the Goober State.

CAPITAL STICKER

FLOWER STICKER

Cherokee Rose

Frankly, my dear . . . Native Georgian Margaret Mitchell's *Gone With the Wind* is a famous novel describing life in the South during the Civil War.

True Trivia:
The civil rights leader Martin Luther King was born in Atlanta, Georgia. King used peaceful protests to help win equality for African-Americans.

Hawaii

☆ The Aloha State ☆

FLAG STICKER

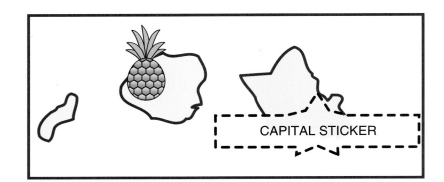

CAPITAL STICKER

Hawaii is the biggest of the Hawaiian islands. It also has one of the world's largest active volcanoes, Mauna Loa.

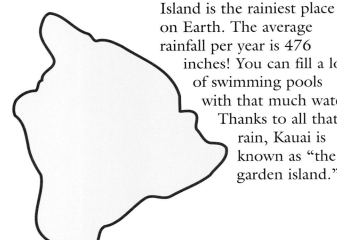

Mt. Waialeale on Kauai Island is the rainiest place on Earth. The average rainfall per year is 476 inches! You can fill a lot of swimming pools with that much water. Thanks to all that rain, Kauai is known as "the garden island."

FLOWER STICKER

Hibiscus

ALOHA

Fun Fact:
Aloha is a Hawaiian word that means both *hello* and *good-bye*!

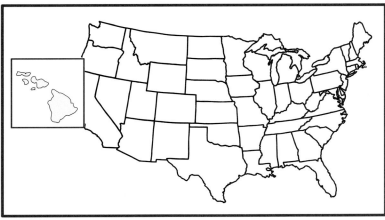

Idaho

☆ The Gem State ☆

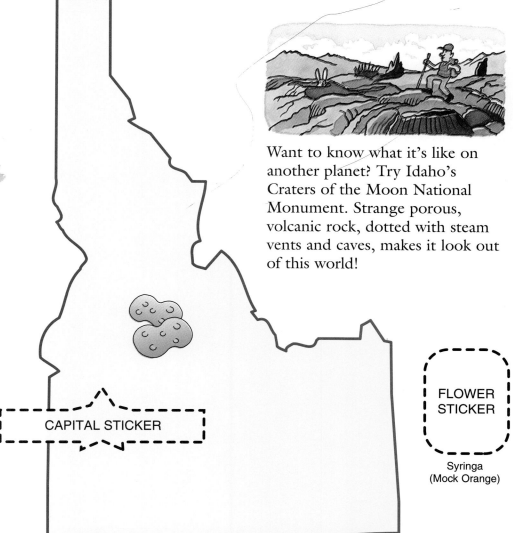

Want to know what it's like on another planet? Try Idaho's Craters of the Moon National Monument. Strange porous, volcanic rock, dotted with steam vents and caves, makes it look out of this world!

The famous explorers Lewis and Clark were the very first non-Indians to visit Idaho. In 1805 Clark started down the Salmon River, but he turned back after 50 miles of churning white water and sudden turns. The Salmon River is so hard to travel that people call it the *River of No Return*.

Syringa
(Mock Orange)

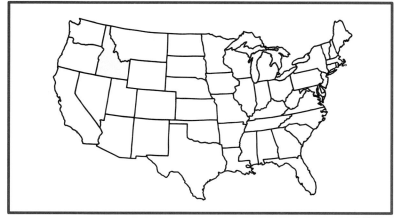

True Trivia:
Idaho is an Indian word meaning *Behold the Light on the Mountains.*

Illinois

☆ The Prairie State ☆

In 1830 the site of what would become Chicago was only a cluster of 20 log cabins. Today Chicago is home to the world's tallest building—the 110-story Sears Tower!

A prairie is a large area of grassland with few, if any, trees. Prairies are known for their rich soil. Many of the prairies in Illinois are now farms that grow soybeans and corn. Prairies are also famous for prairie dogs!

Meadow Violet

Fun Fact:
Abraham Lincoln started his law career in Illinois, which is sometimes called the Land of Lincoln.

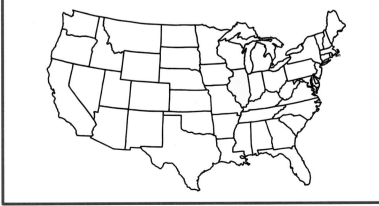

Indiana

☆ The Hoosier State ☆

Indianapolis is the home of the famous Indianapolis 500 car race. Racers in the 500-mile race must drive 200 times around a 2 1/2-mile oval track.

Indiana loves basketball! Indianapolis is the home of the Basketball Hall of Fame, which contains trophies, pictures, and all sorts of other things relating to Indiana's favorite sport.

Peony

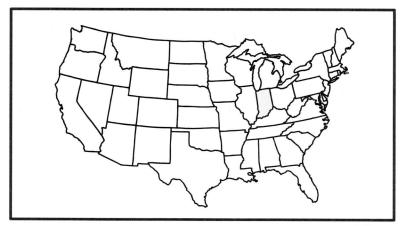

True Trivia: More interstate highways connect in Indianapolis than any other city.

17

Iowa

☆ The Hawkeye State ☆

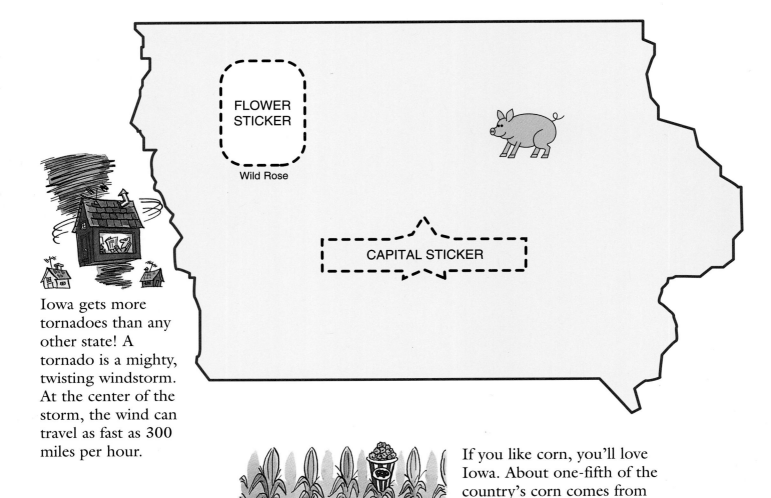

FLAG STICKER

FLOWER STICKER

Wild Rose

CAPITAL STICKER

Iowa gets more tornadoes than any other state! A tornado is a mighty, twisting windstorm. At the center of the storm, the wind can travel as fast as 300 miles per hour.

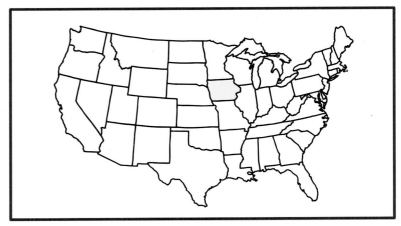

If you like corn, you'll love Iowa. About one-fifth of the country's corn comes from Iowa's rich farmlands.

Fun Fact:
Iowa has the highest literacy rate in the USA. More than 99% of Iowa's citizens can read!

Kansas

☆ The Sunflower State ☆

The Wonderful Wizard of Oz by L. Frank Baum starts and ends with a cyclone and is about Dorothy Gale, from Kansas!

FLAG STICKER

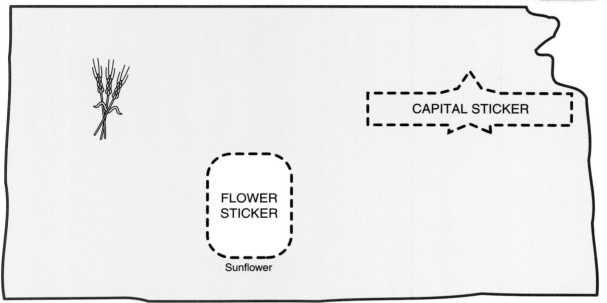

CAPITAL STICKER

FLOWER STICKER

Sunflower

During the days of the Wild West, the cowboys who came through Dodge City, Kansas, liked to kick up their heels. There were often brawls and even gunfights. Wyatt Earp and Bat Masterson were among the famous lawmen who tried to tame Dodge City.

True Trivia:
The geographical center of the 48 neighbor states is near Lebanon, Kansas.

19

Kentucky

☆ The Bluegrass State ☆

Each spring Louisville hosts the USA's oldest continually run horse race—the Kentucky Derby. Before the start of every race, they play "My Old Kentucky Home."

Goldenrod

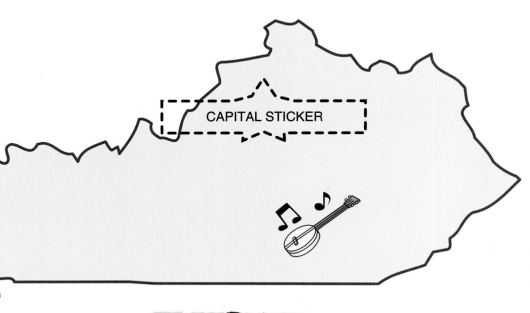

Kentucky comes from a Cherokee word meaning *Land of Tomorrow* or *meadowland*. Kentucky is called the Bluegrass State because of the deep greenish-blue grass that grows there. The toe-tapping folk music of the region is also called bluegrass.

Fun Fact:
Daniel Boone was one of the first white men to explore Kentucky. He founded a settlement called Fort Boonesborough.

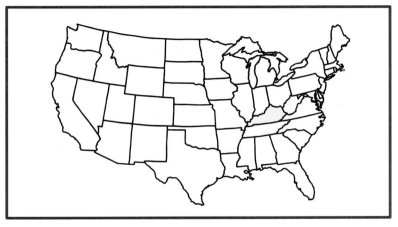

Louisiana

☆ The Pelican State ☆

FLAG STICKER

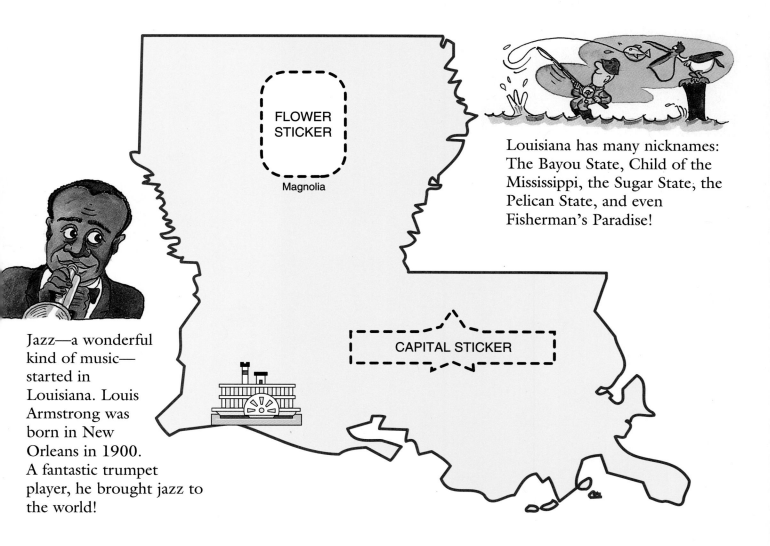

FLOWER STICKER

Magnolia

CAPITAL STICKER

Louisiana has many nicknames: The Bayou State, Child of the Mississippi, the Sugar State, the Pelican State, and even Fisherman's Paradise!

Jazz—a wonderful kind of music—started in Louisiana. Louis Armstrong was born in New Orleans in 1900. A fantastic trumpet player, he brought jazz to the world!

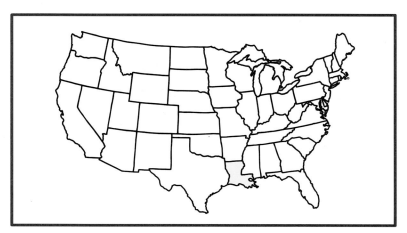

True Trivia:
Mardi Gras is a festival held each year in New Orleans, Louisiana. During Mardi Gras, the people dress up in costumes, go to parades, and dance in the streets!

21

Maine

☆ The Pine Tree State ☆

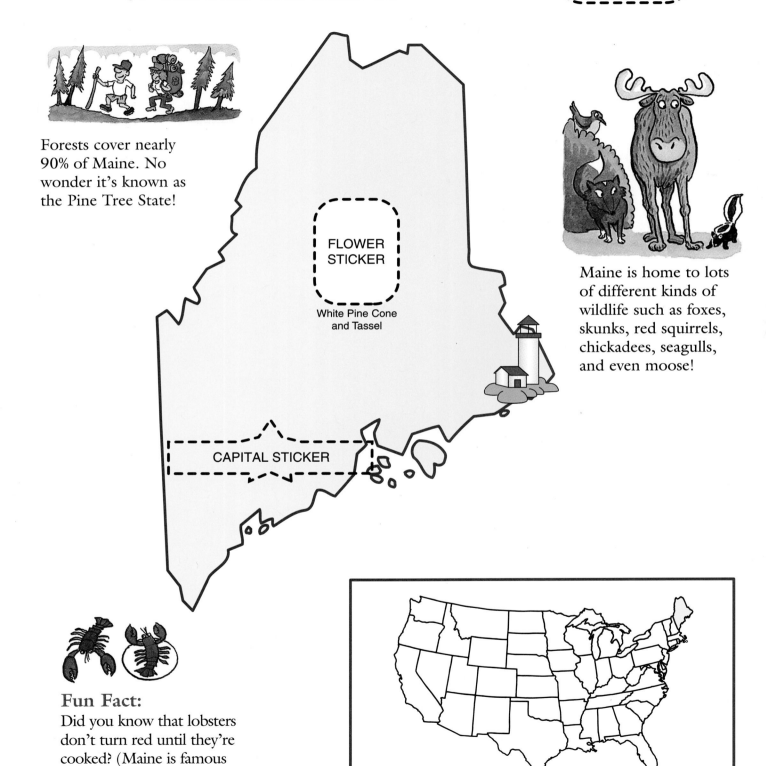

Forests cover nearly 90% of Maine. No wonder it's known as the Pine Tree State!

FLOWER STICKER

White Pine Cone and Tassel

CAPITAL STICKER

Maine is home to lots of different kinds of wildlife such as foxes, skunks, red squirrels, chickadees, seagulls, and even moose!

Fun Fact:
Did you know that lobsters don't turn red until they're cooked? (Maine is famous for its lobsters.)

22

Maryland

☆ The Old Line State ☆

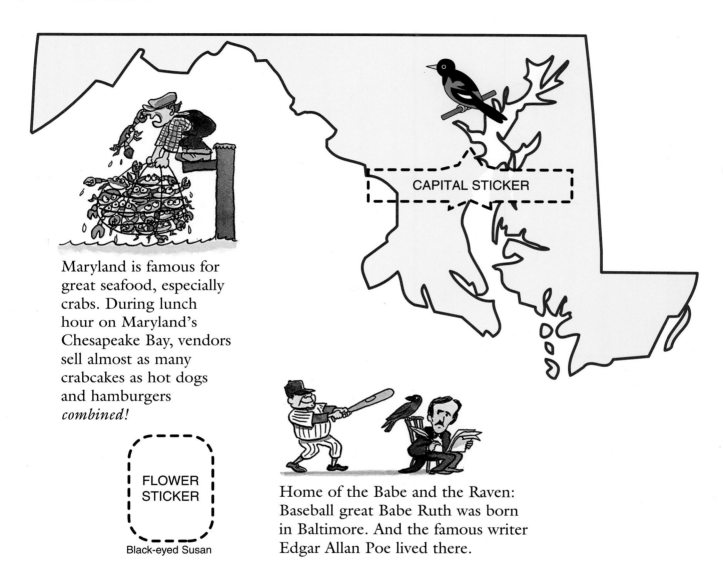

Maryland is famous for great seafood, especially crabs. During lunch hour on Maryland's Chesapeake Bay, vendors sell almost as many crabcakes as hot dogs and hamburgers *combined!*

Black-eyed Susan

Home of the Babe and the Raven: Baseball great Babe Ruth was born in Baltimore. And the famous writer Edgar Allan Poe lived there.

True Trivia:
The state dog is the Chesapeake Bay Retriever. And believe it or not, the state sport of Maryland is jousting!

23

Massachusetts

☆ The Bay State ☆

Paul Revere made his famous ride from Boston to Lexington to report that British troops had closed Boston Harbor.

FLAG STICKER

FLOWER STICKER

Mayflower

CAPITAL STICKER

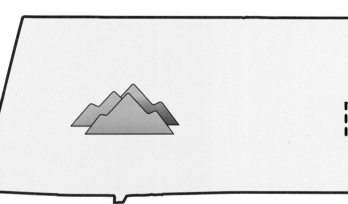

The Pilgrims first came to Massachusetts in 1620 to escape from religious persecution in England. By 1640 there were eight towns in Plymouth Colony!

Fun Facts:

Boston is famous for its many colleges, its annual Marathon, and its baked beans!

Michigan

☆ The Great Lakes State ☆

That's a lot of cars! Detroit, Michigan, produces over one-fifth of all the cars, trucks, and tractors made in the USA so it's sometimes called Motortown. Motown (a shortened pronunciation of Motortown) is also the name for a bouncy kind of music recorded in Detroit.

Michigan is bordered by four of the five Great Lakes: Lake Superior, Lake Huron, Lake Erie, and, of course, Lake Michigan. The lakes divide the land into two peninsulas. A peninsula is a piece of land surrounded by water on three sides.

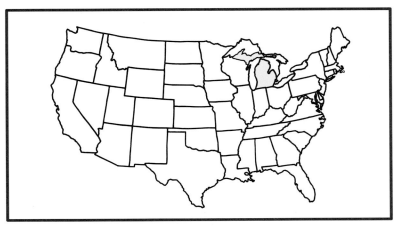

True Trivia:
Michigan is sometimes called the Wolverine State because of the many wolverines who used to roam the area.

Minnesota

☆ The Land of 10,000 Lakes ☆

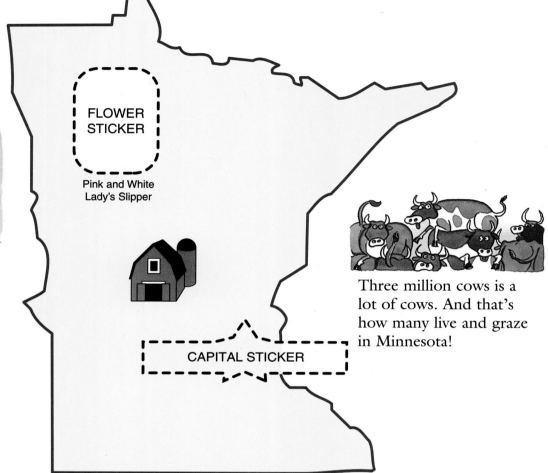

Pink and White Lady's Slipper

Lots of ice—St. Paul's Winter Carnival in early February features ice shows, snowmobile races, and ice sculpture exhibits.

Three million cows is a lot of cows. And that's how many live and graze in Minnesota!

Fun Fact:
For a while the settlement that would become St. Paul was known as Pig's Eye. Why? That was the nickname for a Canadian fur trader who lived there.

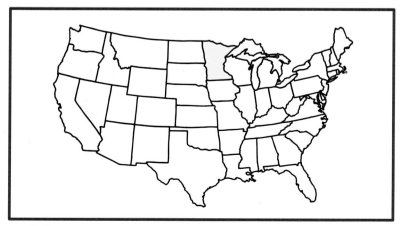

26

Mississippi

☆ The Magnolia State ☆

Officially Mississippi!
Mississippi's state insect is the honeybee. Its state shell is the oyster shell. And its state fossil is the prehistoric whale.

FLOWER STICKER

Magnolia

CAPITAL STICKER

Mississippi was named after the nation's greatest river. Mississippi comes from the Algonquin word *messipi* meaning *gathering in of all waters*. Many smaller streams and rivers empty into the Mississippi.

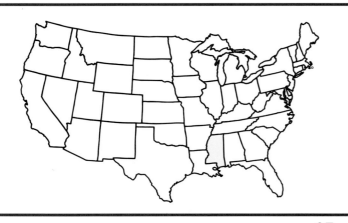

True Trivia:
The capital of Mississippi was named after Andrew Jackson, the seventh president of the U.S.

Missouri

☆ The Show Me State ☆

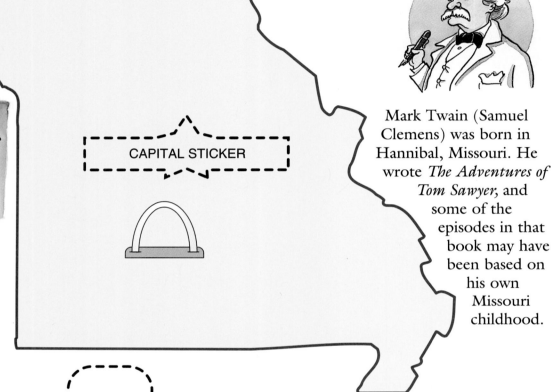

FLAG STICKER

CAPITAL STICKER

In 1927, Charles Lindbergh made a historic flight across the Atlantic Ocean. A group of St. Louis, Missouri, businessmen helped Lindbergh raise the money to buy his plane. To thank them, Lindbergh named his small plane *The Spirit of Saint Louis.*

Mark Twain (Samuel Clemens) was born in Hannibal, Missouri. He wrote *The Adventures of Tom Sawyer,* and some of the episodes in that book may have been based on his own Missouri childhood.

FLOWER STICKER

Hawthorn

Fun Fact:

St. Louis houses the National Bowling Hall of Fame and Museum. If you go there, you can roll 90-year-old bowling balls!

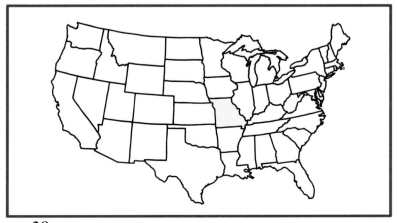

Montana

☆ The Treasure State ☆

Many people have come to Montana to seek their fortunes. Montana's state motto is *Oro y plata*. That means *gold and silver* in Spanish.

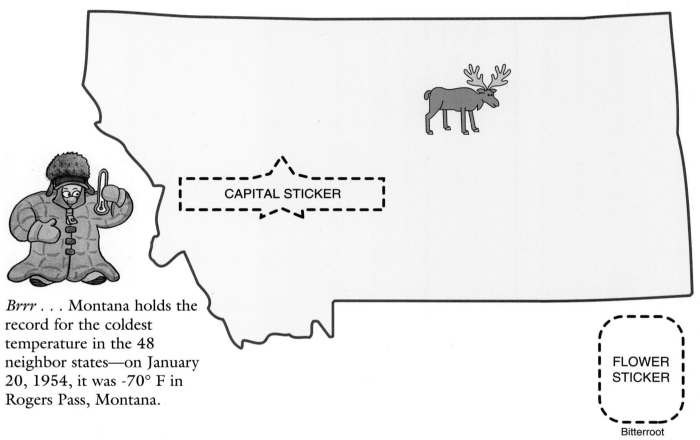

Brrr . . . Montana holds the record for the coldest temperature in the 48 neighbor states—on January 20, 1954, it was -70° F in Rogers Pass, Montana.

Bitterroot

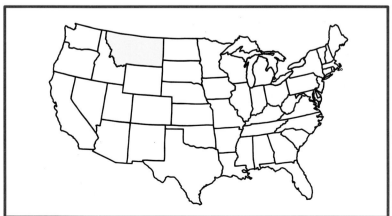

True Trivia:

One of the few bison herds in the USA can be found at The National Bison Range in western Montana.

Nebraska

☆ The Cornhusker State ☆

Pioneers heading west on the Oregon Trail had to cross the vast, flat, seemingly endless plains of Nebraska. Finally the pioneers would see a wonderful sight—a 150-foot-tall rock! Chimney Rock near the North Platte River in western Nebraska marks the end of the "endless" plains.

FLAG STICKER

FLOWER STICKER

Goldenrod

CAPITAL STICKER

Each September Omaha, Nebraska, hosts the World's Championship Rodeo. The rodeo is held at the Ak-Sar-Ben Field and Coliseum. Guess what Ak-Sar-Ben spells backward!

Fun Fact:
Nebraska's capital was named in honor of President Abraham Lincoln.

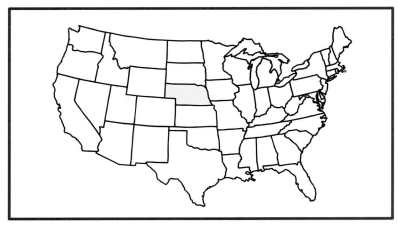

30

Nevada

☆ The Silver State ☆

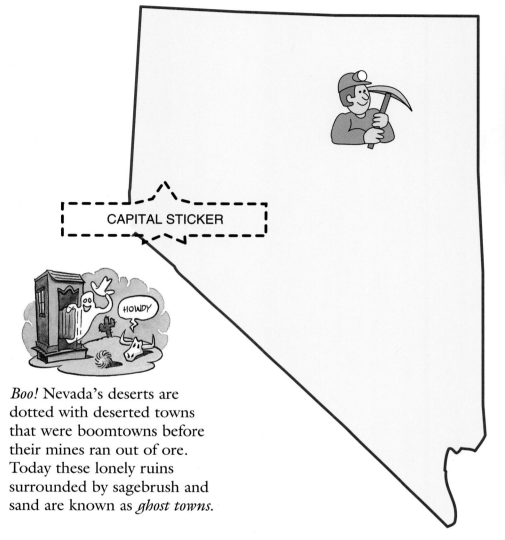

Lake Mead is the largest manmade reservoir in the world. It is formed by the 726-foot-high Hoover Dam, which controls the waters of the mighty Colorado River.

FLAG STICKER

CAPITAL STICKER

FLOWER STICKER

Sagebrush

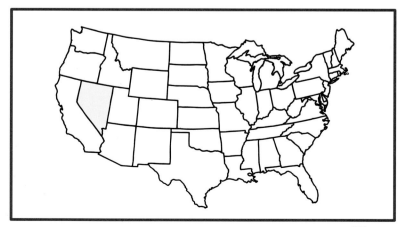

Boo! Nevada's deserts are dotted with deserted towns that were boomtowns before their mines ran out of ore. Today these lonely ruins surrounded by sagebrush and sand are known as *ghost towns.*

True Trivia:
Many people travel to Las Vegas, Nevada, to see the famous nightclubs and casinos.

31

New Hampshire

☆ The Granite State ☆

New Hampshire is a fun place to be all year round. In summer, tourists flock to the state's many beaches and blue lakes. In the winter, skiers swoosh down New Hampshire's White Mountains. Spring brings the return of beautiful greenery. And so many people come to see New Hampshire's brilliant fall foliage that these tourists have a special name: leaf peepers.

FLAG STICKER

WOOSH! The fastest wind speed ever recorded in the USA was on top of New Hampshire's Mt. Washington. In 1934, the wind reached 231 mph!

FLOWER STICKER

Purple Lilac

CAPITAL STICKER

Fun Fact:
Rock hound alert! You can find over 200 kinds of rocks and minerals in New Hampshire.

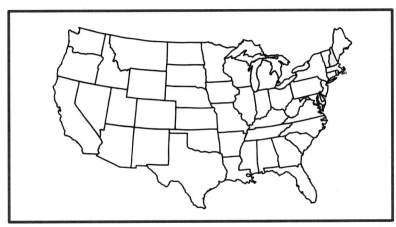

New Jersey

☆ The Garden State ☆

FLAG STICKER

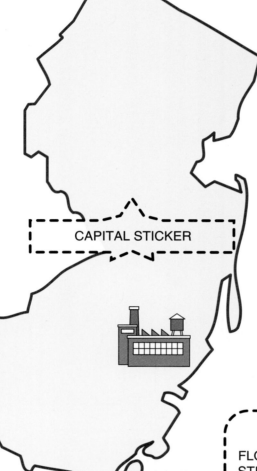

CAPITAL STICKER

What a bright idea! The great inventor Thomas A. Edison lived in New Jersey. Edison worked on many inventions, including movies. But his most famous invention of all was the lightbulb.

New Jersey was home to lots of other famous people, too: Samuel F. B. Morse, the inventor of the telegraph; John P. Holland, who invented the submarine; popular singer Frank Sinatra; Stephen Crane, author of *The Red Badge of Courage*; and James Fenimore Cooper, author of *The Last of the Mohicans*.

FLOWER STICKER

Purple Violet

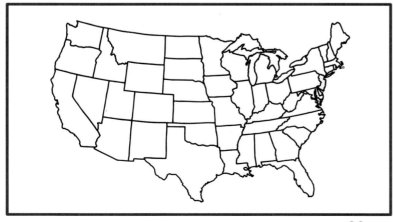

True Trivia:
The British named New Jersey after the Island of Jersey in the English Channel.

33

New Mexico

☆ The Land of Enchantment State ☆

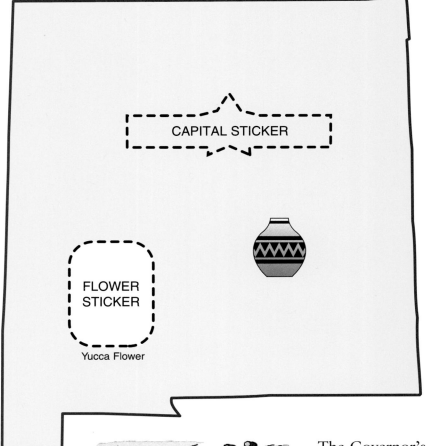

CAPITAL STICKER

FLOWER STICKER

Yucca Flower

FLAG STICKER

Adobe buildings are made from adobe bricks, which consist of clay that is mixed with straw, then dried in the sun. Though the outside temperature may be scorching, the inside of an adobe building stays cool!

The Governor's Palace in Santa Fe is the oldest seat of government in the USA. This beautiful adobe building was built in 1610!

Fun Fact:
The first Europeans to move to this part of the USA were Spaniards looking for gold.

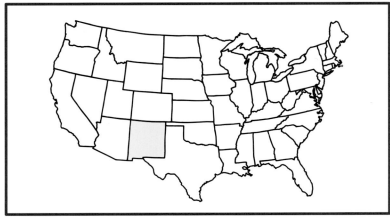

New York

☆ The Empire State ☆

Over 6 million people visit Niagara Falls each year to watch over 200,000 cubic feet of water splash over 167-foot-high cliffs—some even go over in a barrel!

"Give me your tired, your poor, your huddled masses yearning to breathe free." The Statue of Liberty on Liberty Island near Manhattan is a symbol of freedom to immigrants seeking a better life in the USA.

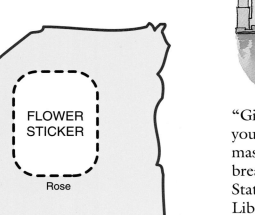

Rose

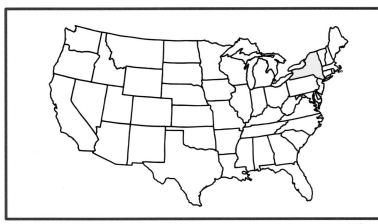

True Trivia:
New York City was once the capital of the USA. George Washington became the first president in NYC.

35

North Carolina

☆ The Tar Heel State ☆

Buzz, buzz . . . During the Revolutionary War, British General Cornwallis called Charlotte, North Carolina, a "hornet's nest" of resistance. Proud of being so hard to defeat, the residents adopted a hornet's nest as the official symbol of their city.

FLAG STICKER

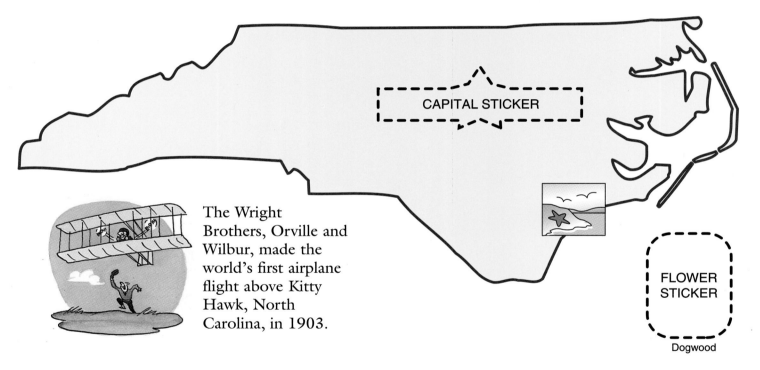

CAPITAL STICKER

The Wright Brothers, Orville and Wilbur, made the world's first airplane flight above Kitty Hawk, North Carolina, in 1903.

FLOWER STICKER

Dogwood

Fun Fact:
Before the California gold rush, North Carolina was the nation's biggest gold producer.

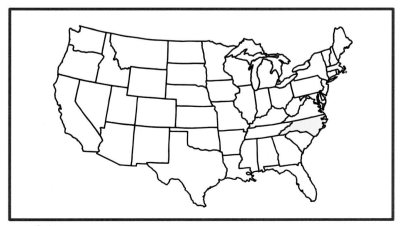

North Dakota

FLAG STICKER

⭐ The Flickertail State ⭐

North Dakota is also known as the Sioux State or Land of the Dakotas. It was named for the native Dakota Sioux tribes. Dakota means *friends* or *allies* in the Sioux language.

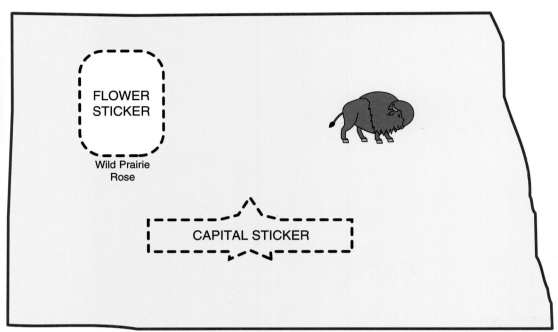

FLOWER STICKER

Wild Prairie Rose

CAPITAL STICKER

Teddy Roosevelt once ran a cattle ranch in North Dakota. As a rancher, he came to respect the rugged badlands. Later as president, Roosevelt worked hard to protect the nation's natural resources, including the badlands.

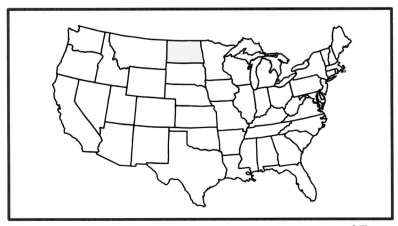

True Trivia:
North Dakota shares the International Peace Garden park with its neighbor Canada.

Ohio

☆ The Buckeye State ☆

GRANT HAYES GARFIELD
HARRISON McKINLEY TAFT
HARDING

Ohio was the birthplace of these modern American presidents: Ulysses S. Grant, Rutherford B. Hayes, James Garfield, Benjamin Harrison, William McKinley, William H. Taft, and Warren G. Harding.

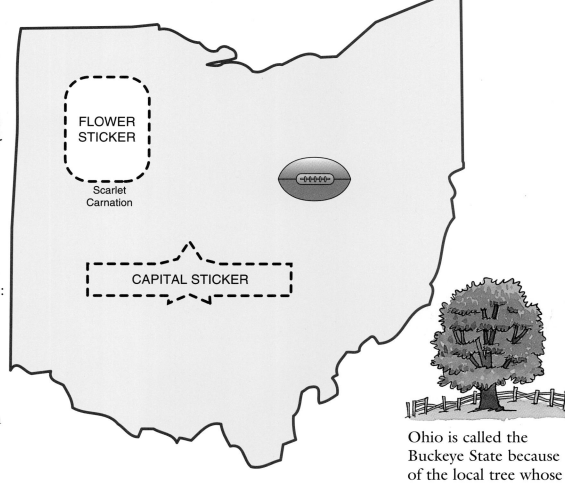

FLOWER STICKER

Scarlet Carnation

CAPITAL STICKER

Ohio is called the Buckeye State because of the local tree whose nut looks like the open eye of a deer.

WELCOME

Fun Fact:
Cincinnati's famous zoo includes America's first insectarium—
a zoo just for bugs!

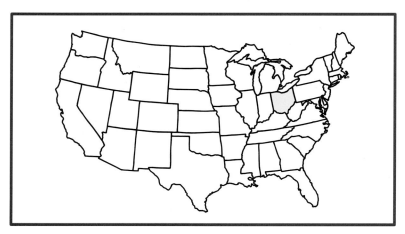

Oklahoma

FLAG STICKER

In 1928 oil was discovered in Oklahoma City. Today there are even oil wells on the lawn of the capitol building!

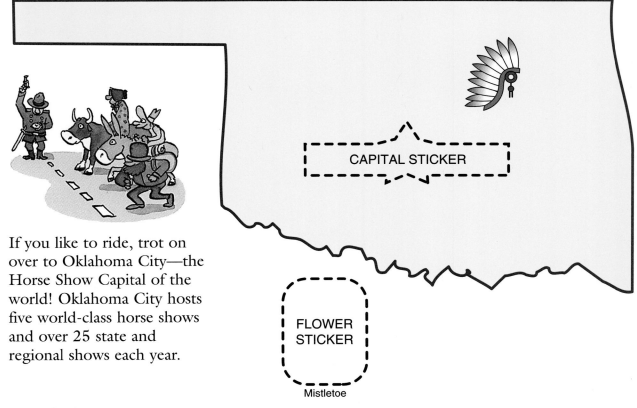

CAPITAL STICKER

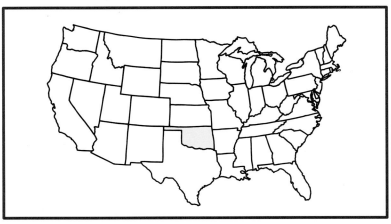

If you like to ride, trot on over to Oklahoma City—the Horse Show Capital of the world! Oklahoma City hosts five world-class horse shows and over 25 state and regional shows each year.

FLOWER STICKER

Mistletoe

True Trivia:
The famous cowboy, singer, and comedian Will Rogers hailed from Oklahoma.

Oregon

☆ The Beaver State ☆

The settlers who founded Portland were Francis Pettygrove of Portland, Maine, and Asa Lovejoy of Boston, Massachusetts. They couldn't agree on what to call the new city, so they tossed a coin. Guess who won?

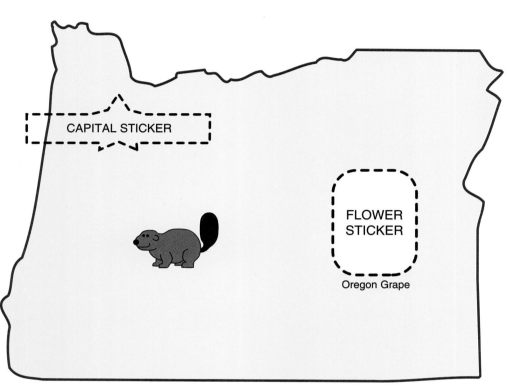

CAPITAL STICKER

FLOWER STICKER

Oregon Grape

One day about 7,700 years ago, a huge volcano erupted and its top collapsed. A lake was formed. That beautiful, dark blue lake is now at the center of Oregon's Crater Lake National Park.

Fun Fact:
Every year Portland throws a 24-day long party—the rose festival.

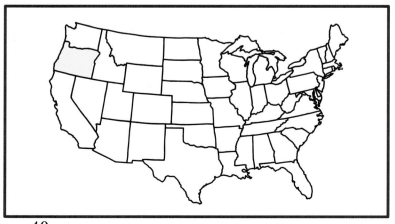

Pennsylvania

☆ The Keystone State ☆

FLAG STICKER

FLOWER STICKER

Mountain Laurel

CAPITAL STICKER

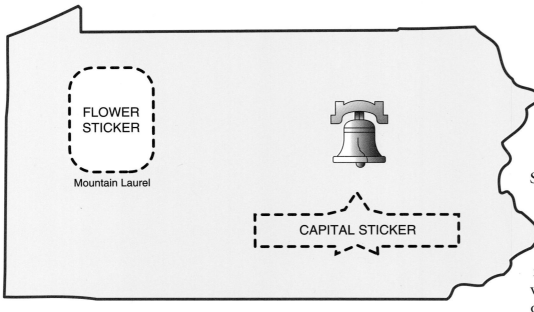

Statesman, scientist, writer, and inventor Ben Franklin was born in Massachusetts but moved to Philadelphia when he was 17 years old. Ben Franklin formed the first Pennsylvania fire department.

Philadelphia, Pennsylvania, was a very important city in colonial times. Both the Declaration of Independence and the Constitution were signed in Philadelphia. Philadelphia was the nation's capital from 1790 to 1800. Philadelphia is the largest city in Pennsylvania.

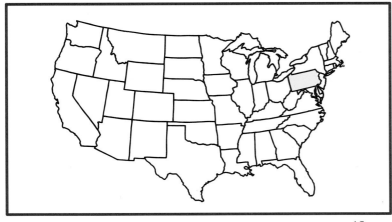

True Trivia:
William Penn wanted to call his land *Sylvania*, which is Latin for woodlands. Pennsylvania means *Penn's Woods.*

Rhode Island

☆ The Ocean State ☆

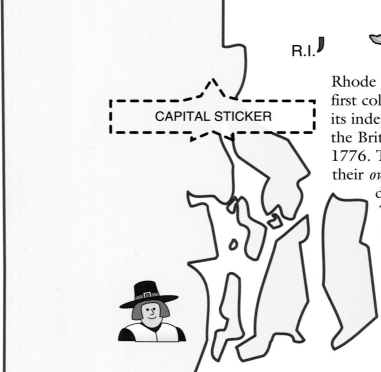

R.I.

AL.

The origin of Rhode Island's name is not certain. The Dutch explorer Adriaen Block might have called it Roodt Eylandt, meaning *red island*, because of the state's reddish soil.

Rhode Island was the first colony to declare its independence from the British Crown in 1776. They celebrate their *own* independence day on May 4! This spirited state is the smallest in the USA. Alaska is almost 425 times bigger than Rhode Island.

Violet

I'M A YANKEE DOODLE DANDY

Fun Fact:

The composer George M. Cohan was born in Providence, Rhode Island, in 1878. He wrote "Yankee Doodle Dandy."

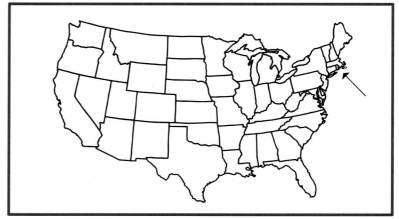

South Carolina

☆ The Palmetto State ☆

FLAG STICKER

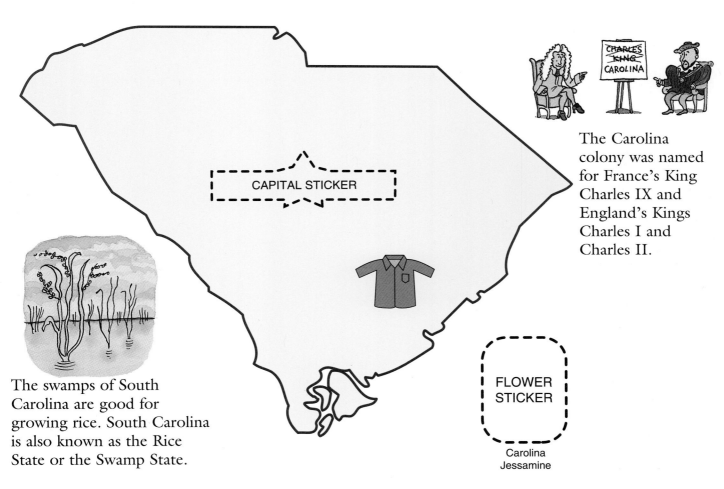

CAPITAL STICKER

The Carolina colony was named for France's King Charles IX and England's Kings Charles I and Charles II.

The swamps of South Carolina are good for growing rice. South Carolina is also known as the Rice State or the Swamp State.

FLOWER STICKER

Carolina Jessamine

IT'S HOME TO ME

True Trivia:
A swamp is wet, spongy land that is often covered partly by water. Frogs love swamps!

South Dakota

☆ The Coyote State ☆

The faces carved into South Dakota's Mt. Rushmore belong to four presidents: George Washington, Thomas Jefferson, Theodore Roosevelt, and Abraham Lincoln. The carvings average 60 feet from top of the head to chin. That's taller than a four-story building!

FLAG STICKER

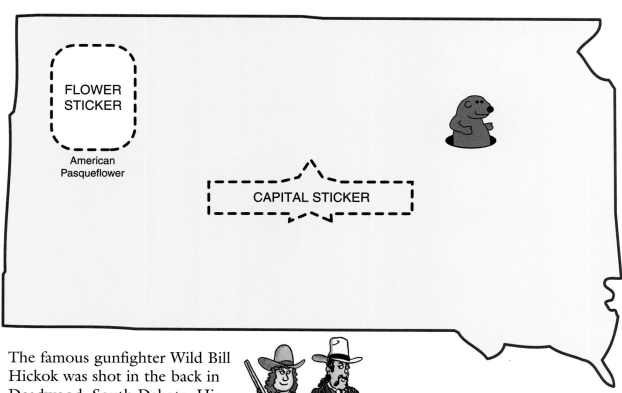

FLOWER STICKER

American Pasqueflower

CAPITAL STICKER

The famous gunfighter Wild Bill Hickok was shot in the back in Deadwood, South Dakota. His friend Calamity Jane is buried beside him.

Fun Fact:
90% of South Dakota is covered with ranches and farms.

Tennessee

Each August, Memphis holds a citywide celebration honoring the King of Rock 'N' Roll—Elvis Presley.

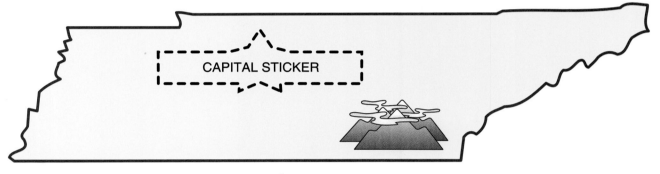

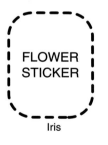

Yee-ha! Nashville, Tennessee, is the country music capital of the world. The greatest stars of country music perform at Nashville's famous Grand Ole Opry.

Iris

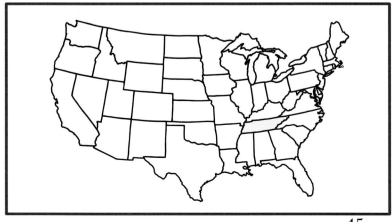

True Trivia: President Andrew Jackson named Memphis after a city in Egypt.

Texas

☆ The Lone Star State ☆

FLAG STICKER

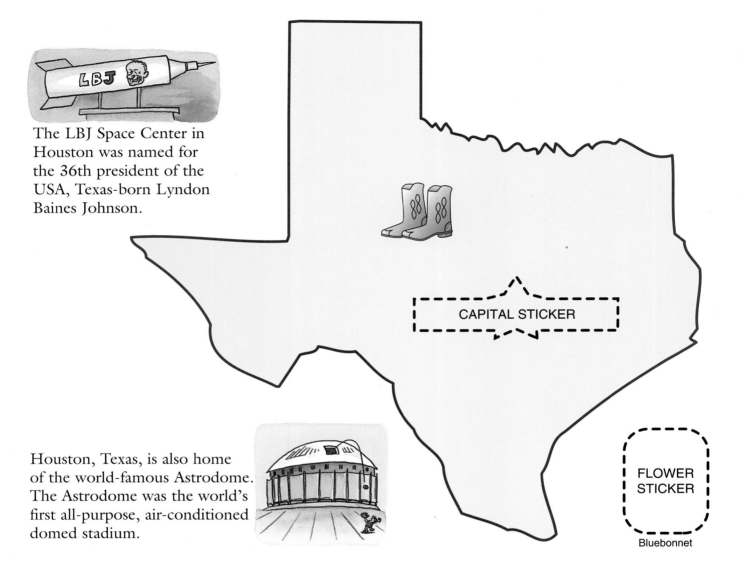

The LBJ Space Center in Houston was named for the 36th president of the USA, Texas-born Lyndon Baines Johnson.

CAPITAL STICKER

FLOWER STICKER

Bluebonnet

Houston, Texas, is also home of the world-famous Astrodome. The Astrodome was the world's first all-purpose, air-conditioned domed stadium.

Fun Fact:
Texas comes from the Caddo Indian word *Texas* or *Teysha*, which means *Hello, friend*.

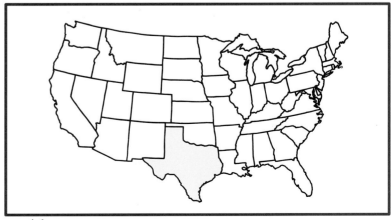

46

Utah

 ⭐ The Beehive State ⭐

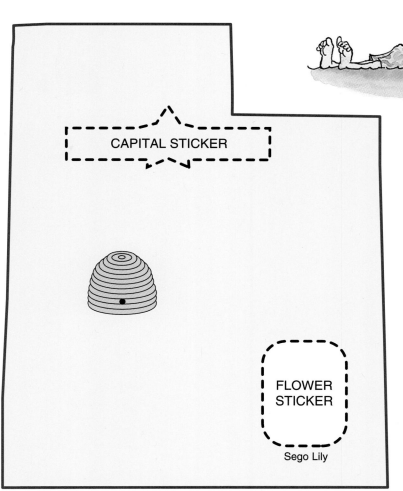

CAPITAL STICKER

FLOWER STICKER

Sego Lily

Landscape Arch is 291 feet from one end to the other and rises about 100 feet above the ground. You can find it in Arches National Park along with many other amazing rock formations.

Salt Lake City is near a lake that is so salty, swimmers float above the water like corks! Salt Lake is several *times* saltier than seawater.

True Trivia:
The biggest dinosaur footprints in the world are in Utah. The prints belonged to a *hadrosaurid* (duckbill).

Vermont

⭐ The Green Mountain State ⭐

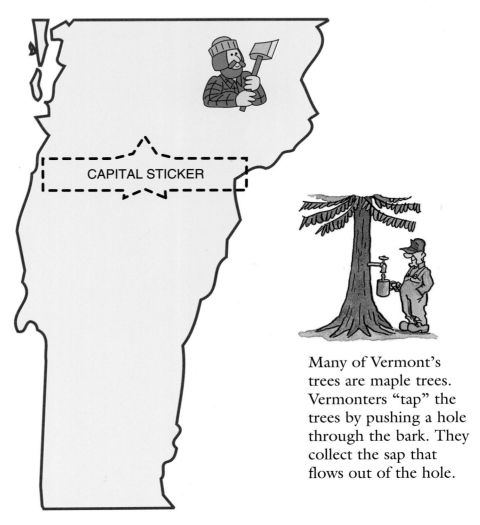

Most of Vermont is covered by forest. Not very many people live there, but tourists love visiting Vermont to go skiing!

Red Clover

Many of Vermont's trees are maple trees. Vermonters "tap" the trees by pushing a hole through the bark. They collect the sap that flows out of the hole.

Fun Fact:
The sap from maple trees is boiled until it thickens into maple syrup and maple sugar candy!

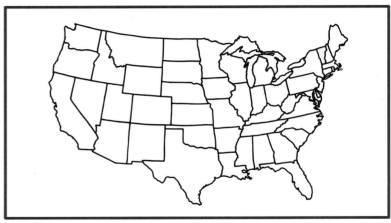

Virginia

★ The Old Dominion State ★

In Arlington, Virginia, you can find the Tomb of the Unknown Soldier. This monument honors the fallen from many American wars.

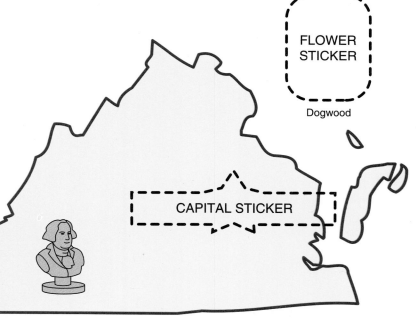

CAPITAL STICKER

Williamsburg, Virginia, looks exactly like a town from colonial times. Costumed guides show visitors how people lived in colonial Williamsburg. Many of the buildings there were actually built in colonial days!

True Trivia:
Virginia was the first permanent English settlement in the New World.

Washington

☆ The Evergreen State ☆

Our very own rain forest . . . Washington's Olympic National Park receives over 100 inches of rain per year! Some of its trees are over 300 feet tall.

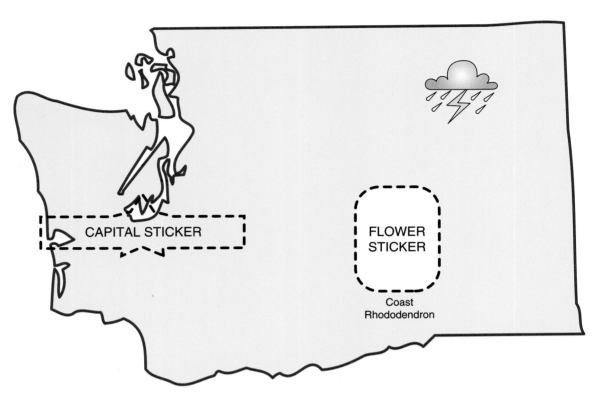

CAPITAL STICKER

FLOWER STICKER

Coast Rhododendron

Mt. Rainier is a dormant volcano. The last time it erupted was in 1969. But nearby is Mt. St. Helens, which erupted many times in 1989. Ash from Mt. St. Helens fell as far away as Maine!

Fun Fact:
Washington is the *only* state named after a president. Guess which one!

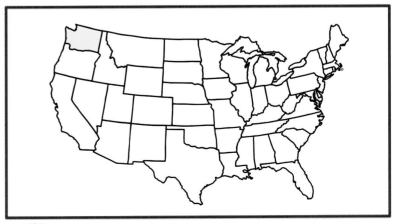

West Virginia

☆ The Mountain State ☆

FLAG STICKER

FLOWER STICKER

Rhododendron

West Virginia became a separate state on the eve of the Civil War. The rest of Virginia decided to leave the Union, while the parts that are now West Virginia chose to stay.

CAPITAL STICKER

West Virginia is the leading coal producer in the USA. What is coal? Coal is a natural fuel. Some people burn coal to heat their homes. To find coal, people dig deep holes called *mines*. The people who work in mines are called *miners*.

True Trivia:
West Virginia's state symbol is a black bear! *Grrr . . .*

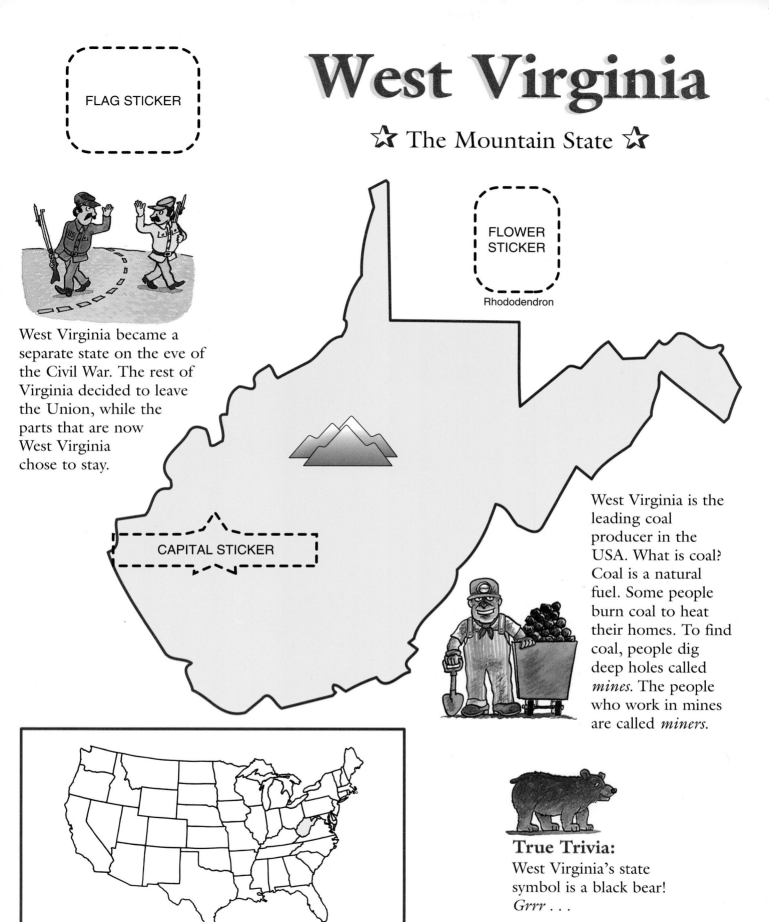

51

Wisconsin

☆ The Badger State ☆

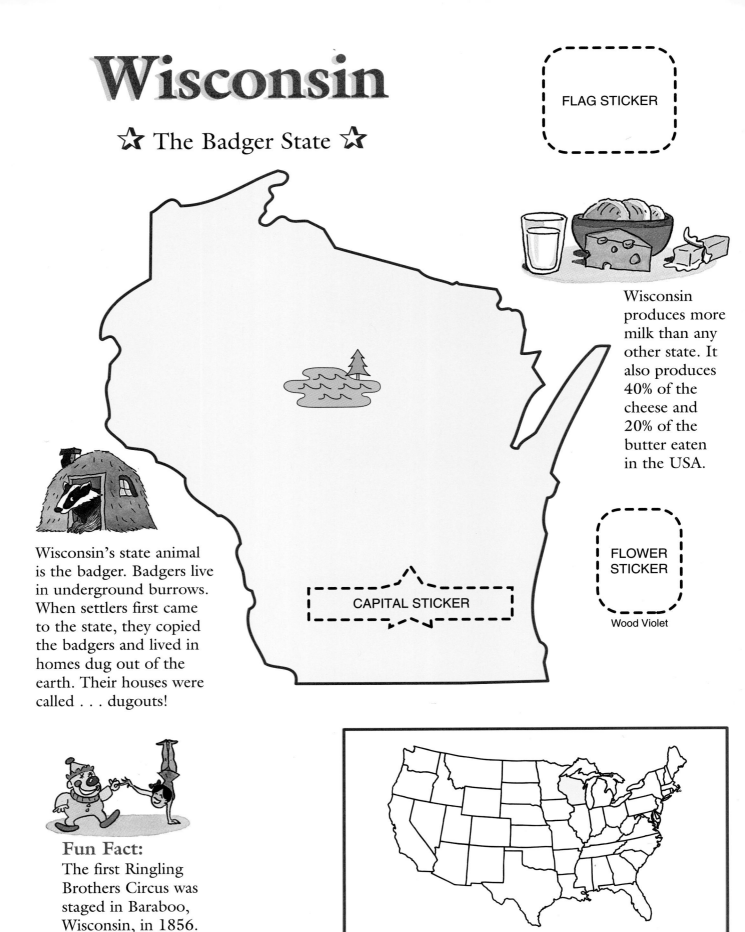

FLAG STICKER

Wisconsin produces more milk than any other state. It also produces 40% of the cheese and 20% of the butter eaten in the USA.

FLOWER STICKER

Wood Violet

CAPITAL STICKER

Wisconsin's state animal is the badger. Badgers live in underground burrows. When settlers first came to the state, they copied the badgers and lived in homes dug out of the earth. Their houses were called . . . dugouts!

Fun Fact:
The first Ringling Brothers Circus was staged in Baraboo, Wisconsin, in 1856.

FLAG STICKER

Wyoming

☆ The Equality State ☆

FLOWER
STICKER

Indian Paintbrush

There are over 200 geysers in Yellowstone. Geysers are springs that shoot hot water into the air. Old Faithful can shoot 10,000 gallons of water into the air during a 5-minute eruption.

CAPITAL STICKER

Yellowstone National Park is home to bears, deer, moose, bighorn sheep, bison, elk, and many other animals.

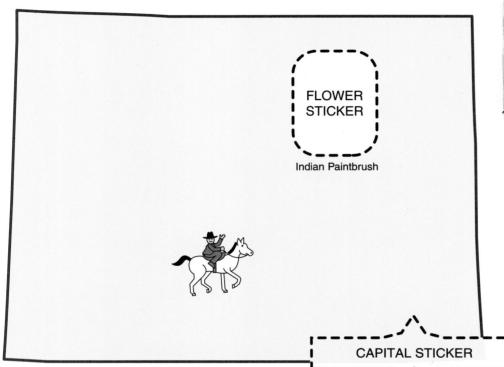

True Trivia:
Wyoming was the first state to give women the vote. That's why it's called The Equality State.

Capital Match Game

Here are all the states and their capitals. Read the lists carefully. Then cover up the capitals and see how many you can remember without peeking!

States	Capitals
Alabama	Montgomery
Alaska	Juneau
Arizona	Phoenix
Arkansas	Little Rock
California	Sacramento
Colorado	Denver
Connecticut	Hartford
Delaware	Dover
Florida	Tallahassee
Georgia	Atlanta
Hawaii	Honolulu
Idaho	Boise
Illinois	Springfield
Indiana	Indianapolis
Iowa	Des Moines
Kansas	Topeka
Kentucky	Frankfort
Louisiana	Baton Rouge
Maine	Augusta
Maryland	Annapolis
Massachusetts	Boston
Michigan	Lansing
Minnesota	St. Paul
Mississippi	Jackson
Missouri	Jefferson City

Montana	Helena
Nebraska	Lincoln
Nevada	Carson City
New Hampshire	Concord
New Jersey	Trenton
New Mexico	Santa Fe
New York	Albany
North Carolina	Raleigh
North Dakota	Bismarck
Ohio	Columbus
Oklahoma	Oklahoma City
Oregon	Salem
Pennsylvania	Harrisburg
Rhode Island	Providence
South Carolina	Columbia
South Dakota	Pierre
Tennessee	Nashville
Texas	Austin
Utah	Salt Lake City
Vermont	Montpelier
Virginia	Richmond
Washington	Olympia
West Virginia	Charleston
Wisconsin	Madison
Wyoming	Cheyenne

Extra Credit:

Can you name the capital of the United States of America? (Hint: It's not a state, but it has almost the same name as one.)

Answer: Washington, D.C.

National Holidays

Citizens of the USA celebrate many different holidays. Some honor important events or people in US history. Draw lines to connect each holiday to its date and meaning.

Columbus Day

The first Monday in September marks the end of summer and honors working people. This holiday is celebrated with parades, picnics, and . . . no work!

Thanksgiving

The second Monday in October honors the European explorer who discovered America.

The third Monday in February honors the births of George Washington and Abraham Lincoln.

Flag Day

On the fourth Thursday in November, Americans enjoy a harvest festival. This holiday was first celebrated in 1621 by the Pilgrims and their Indian friends.

Patriots' Day

June 14, 1777, is the day when Congress voted to adopt our national symbol. This holiday recalls that historic occasion.

Presidents' Day

The third Monday in April recalls Paul Revere's midnight ride to warn the colonial Minutemen that British troops were coming.

Labor Day

Memorial Day

April 22 is a day when many people plant trees. The holiday was started in Nebraska in 1872 by a newspaperman who understood the importance of trees to the land.

Independence Day

Each February 2nd, people check to see if a groundhog sees his shadow and runs back into his underground den. If he does, some people believe there will be six more weeks of winter. If not, they believe spring will come soon.

Arbor Day

The last Monday in May is a holiday honoring the Americans who died in war.

Veterans Day

This holiday was first known as Armistice Day to mark the signing of the peace (Armistice) treaty that ended World War I. The name was changed in 1954 so the holiday could honor all people who served in the Armed Forces during any war.

Groundhog Day

On July 4th, Americans remember how their colonial leaders declared independence from England in 1776.

Election Day

January 15th was the birthday of a great civil rights leader, whose nonviolent work to bring about equality for all people earned him a Nobel Peace Prize.

Martin Luther King Day

The first Tuesday after the first Monday in November is a day set aside for choosing our nation's leaders.

This Land Is Farm Land

The USA is a very big country—3,615,122 square miles, to be exact! That's over 38 times as big as England. There are over 2 million farms in the USA, covering some 991,000,000 acres of land. The wheat fields of the Midwest are so productive that the USA can export grain to many other countries. That is why the USA is sometimes called "the bread basket of the world."

Some American farms grow fruits, vegetables, and grains. Others raise animals such as cows, sheep, and pigs.

THAT'S A LOT OF EGGS.

True Trivia:
US farms produce about
69,476,000,000 eggs a year!

What Time Is It?

People set their clocks and watches according to the sun. The USA is so big that the sun may be up in Maine while it's still pitch dark in California. The USA spans four different time zones: Eastern Standard Time, Central Standard Time, Mountain Time, and Pacific Time. Pacific Time is three hours earlier than Eastern Standard Time. If it is 4 o'clock in New York (Eastern Standard Time), then it is 1 o'clock in California (Pacific Time).

National Symbols

The largest game bird in the USA is the Wild Turkey. These tasty fowl can fly up to 55mph, outrun a fox or dog, and can even swim. (Now that's fast food!) In 1776, Ben Franklin proposed making the Wild Turkey the national symbol. Luckily, the heroic-looking Bald Eagle was chosen instead. Bald Eagles aren't bald. Their heads and necks are covered in white feathers, which make them look bald from a distance.

As the English colonies in the New World grew, each created its own flag. The first colonial flag representing all the colonies together was flown at the battle of Bunker Hill near Boston. It had the cross of the British flag in the upper left, with 13 red and white stripes for the 13 colonies.

In 1777, the first Continental Congress voted that the flag of the United States should have 13 white stars on a blue field, one star for each colony, as well as 13 red and white stripes. Then more colonies joined the Union. So in 1818, Congress voted to keep the number of stripes at 13, but to add one star for every new state. The stars would be added on the July 4th after the state joined the union. The last new star was added on July 4, 1960, to represent Hawaii. Flag Day is celebrated every June 14 in honor of the day in 1777 when Congress voted to make the stars and stripes the American flag.

From Sea to Shining Sea

The West Coast of the USA touches the largest ocean in the world, the Pacific Ocean. The East Coast touches the second largest ocean in the world, the Atlantic. Together these two oceans cover over one-half of the world's surface!

The USA shares five big lakes with its northern neighbor, Canada. The Great Lakes are the largest group of lakes in the world! They are: Lake Superior, Lake Huron, Lake Erie, Lake Ontario, and Lake Michigan. Together the Great Lakes cover 96,000 square miles.

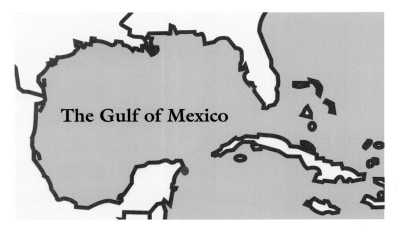

The USA also touches the largest gulf on Earth. The 580,000-square-mile Gulf of Mexico has a 3,100-mile shoreline extending from Cape Sable, Florida, to Cabo Catoche, Mexico.

True Trivia:

The longest river in the USA is the 2,348-mile-long Mississippi River. The Mississippi River winds through 10 states before it empties into the Gulf of Mexico.

A Capital Idea!

The capital of the United States is Washington, D.C. Washington is famous for lots of reasons. Many important government buildings are in Washington, and the president of the United States lives and works there. The president lives in a big house located at 1600 Pennsylvania Avenue—The White House! Every president except for George Washington has lived there.

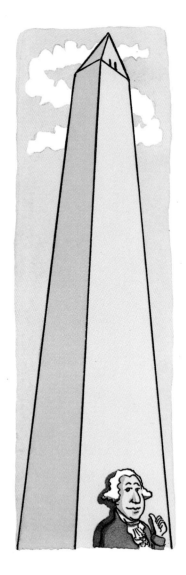

Washington is also known for its many monuments, such as the Lincoln Memorial, the Jefferson Memorial, and the Washington Monument. These monuments honor three of our most famous presidents.

Many people go to Washington to explore its world-famous museums. And in the springtime, Washington attracts thousands of tourists with its Cherry Blossom Festival. Every year millions of people from all over the world visit Washington for its historic sites and beautiful scenery.

The American People

The first people to live in the USA were the Native Americans. The Native Americans, also called Indians, did not divide the land into states. They lived in tribes. Many places in the USA have names taken from Indian words or tribe names. Here are some cities with Indian names: Miami, Yuma, Wichita, Biloxi, and Cheyenne. Can you think of more?

Immigrants are people who come from one country to live in another. People from all over the world come to live together in peace and freedom in the USA.

Immigrants bring their native languages, music, art, food, clothes, and customs. That's why the USA is like many great countries rolled into one!

One group of people did not come to the USA by choice. Many Africans were brought to the US to be sold as slaves. Slavery was finally abolished by the 13th Amendment to the Constitution in 1865.

Welcome To America

For millions of immigrants, Ellis Island was the first American land that they ever saw. For over 60 years Ellis Island was a United States immigration station. Over 12 million immigrants were examined by the officials there. Because so many people entered the United States through Ellis Island, it was nicknamed "The gateway to the New World." Today people are still going to the Island, but for a very different reason. In 1976 Ellis Island was opened to the public as a tourist attraction. Millions of people visit Ellis Island, which is located in the New York Harbor just a few hundred feet from The Statue of Liberty, to learn about the history of the American immigrant.

Fun Fact:

English is the most frequently used language in the USA. But many people who live here speak other languages, too. Because of this, English is constantly changing. Many of the words in the dictionary today came from other countries. Pizza, taco, perfume, kangaroo, karate, and frankfurter are all words that came from other languages.

The National Anthem

The Star-Spangled Banner

Oh, say can you see
    by the dawn's early light,
What so proudly we hailed
    at the twilight's last gleaming?
Whose broad stripes and bright stars
    through the perilous fight,
    O'er the ramparts we watched
    were so gallantly streaming?
And the rocket's red glare,
    the bombs bursting in air,
Gave proof through the night that our
    flag was still there.
Oh, say does that star-spangled banner
    yet wave
O'er the land of the free and the home
    of the brave?

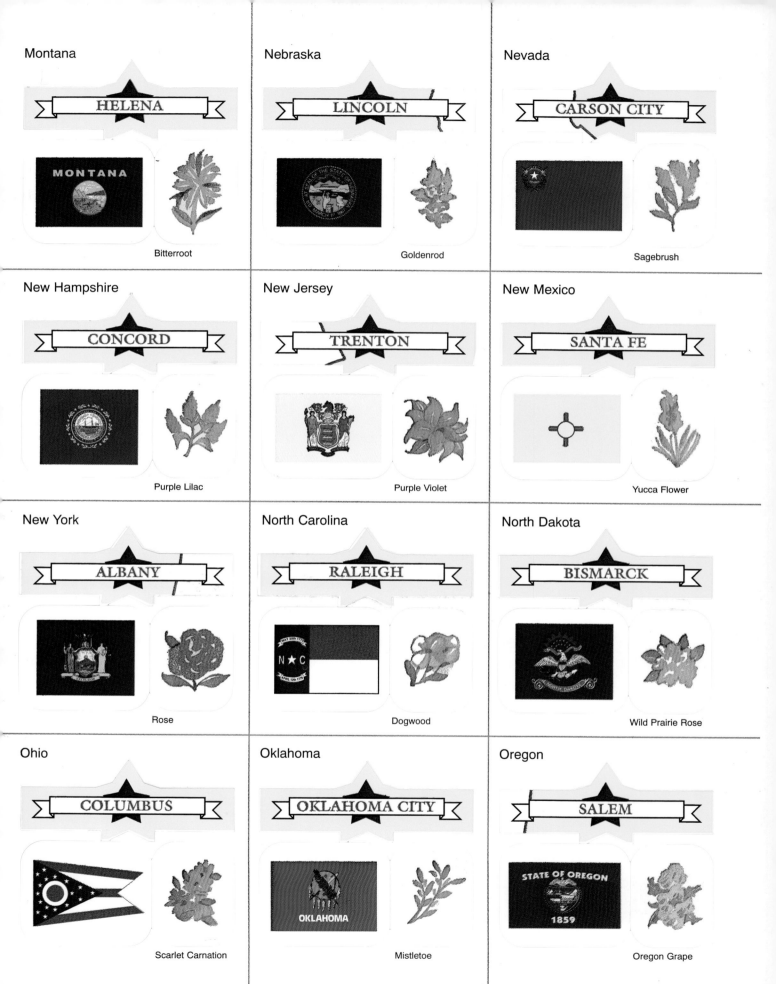

Montana	Nebraska	Nevada
HELENA	LINCOLN	CARSON CITY
Bitterroot	Goldenrod	Sagebrush
New Hampshire	New Jersey	New Mexico
CONCORD	TRENTON	SANTA FE
Purple Lilac	Purple Violet	Yucca Flower
New York	North Carolina	North Dakota
ALBANY	RALEIGH	BISMARCK
Rose	Dogwood	Wild Prairie Rose
Ohio	Oklahoma	Oregon
COLUMBUS	OKLAHOMA CITY	SALEM
Scarlet Carnation	Mistletoe	Oregon Grape

Pennsylvania HARRISBURG Mountain Laurel	**Rhode Island** PROVIDENCE Violet	**South Carolina** COLUMBIA Carolina Jessamine
South Dakota PIERRE American Pasqueflower	**Tennessee** NASHVILLE Iris	**Texas** AUSTIN Bluebonnet
Utah SALT LAKE CITY Sego Lily	**Vermont** MONTPELIER Red Clover	**Virginia** RICHMOND Dogwood
Washington OLYMPIA Coast Rhododendron	**West Virginia** CHARLESTON Rhododendron	**Wisconsin** MADISON Wood Violet

 Wyoming Indian Paintbrush

 CHEYENNE